Diesing

First published in the United States by Silver Burdett Press, 1989

English adaptation © 1989 Silver Burdett Press

All rights reserved including the right of reproduction in whole or in part in any form.

Collection dirigée par Martine et Daniel Sassier

© 1988 by Editions des Deux Coqs d'Or, Paris

Library of Congress Cataloging-in-Publication Data

Poth, Cathy.
    Air / English text, Cathy Poth.
      p. cm.—(Look & learn)
    Adaptation of: L'air / Pierre Avérous.
    Includes index.
    Summary: Discusses air as wind, something to be breathed, a part of the weather, a layer around Earth, and a useful conveyor.
    1. Air—Juvenile literature. [1. Air.] I. Avérous, Pierre, 1946- Air. II. Title. III. Series: Poth, Cathy. Look & learn.
QC161.2.P67   1989
533'.6—dc20   89-6161
                                                        CIP
                                                        AC

ISBN 0-382-09828-5 (lib. bdg.)
ISBN 0-382-09829-3 (pbk.)

The Air

Illustrations by Catherine de Seabra
Adapted by Cathy Poth from an
original French text by Pierre Avérous

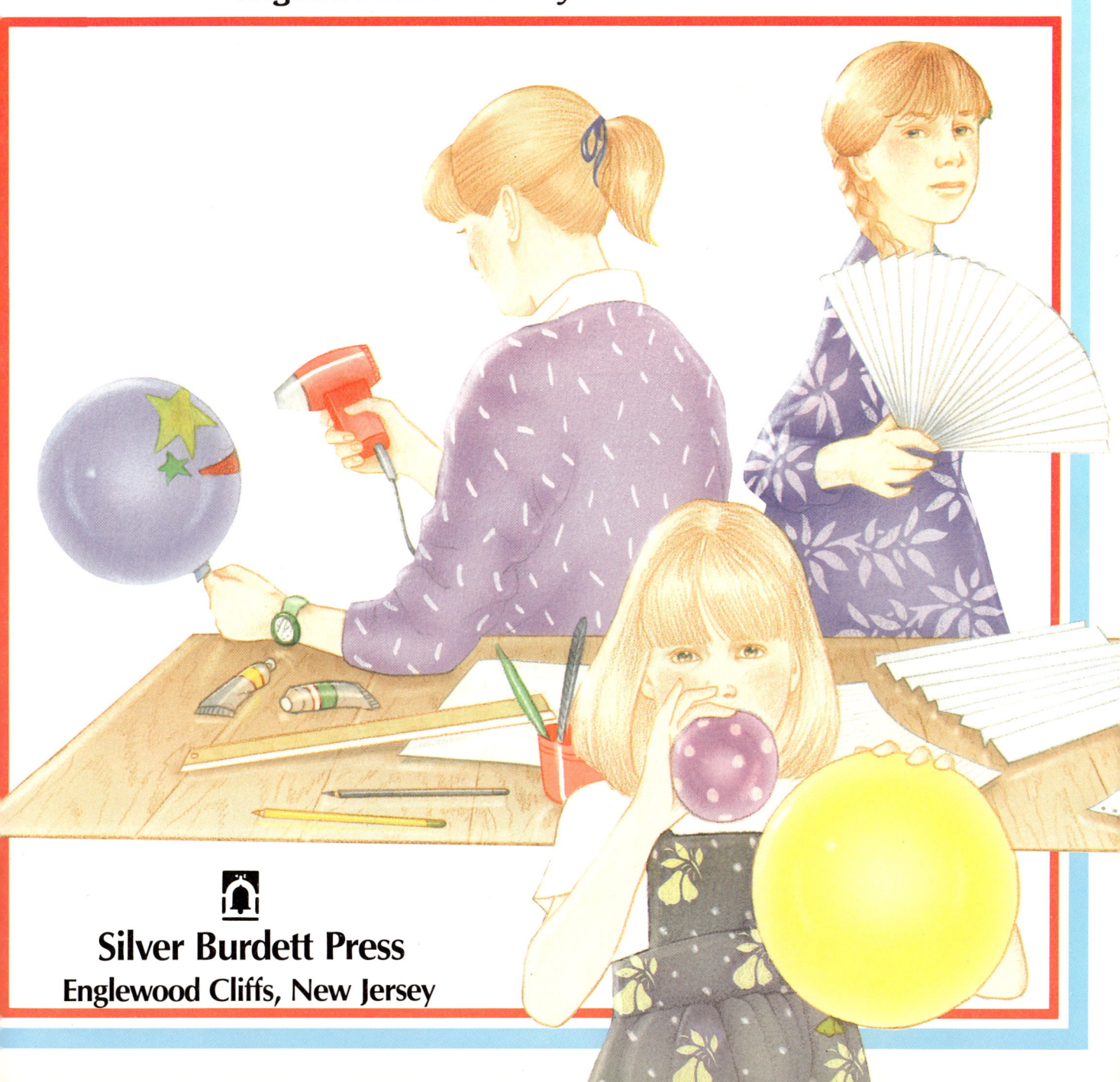

Silver Burdett Press
Englewood Cliffs, New Jersey

Table of Contents

THE WIND   8

- What Is Wind?
- Invisible Air
- The Wind Makes Changes
- A Windsock
- Sails Need Wind
- Hurricanes

AIR TRAVELERS   12

- A Giant Kite
- Easy Flying
- Wings
- Airplanes
- A Pointed Nose
- Falling Slowly

THE AIR WE BREATHE   16

- What's in Air?
- Always Breathing
- Animals Breathe, Too
- Fresh Air
- Plants Need Air
- Fish Don't Like Air

WEATHER IN THE AIR   20

- Hot Air and Cold Air
- Water in the Air
- Beautiful Rainbows
- The Color of the Sky
- A Flash of Lightning
- Weather Instruments

THE ATMOSPHERE: A THICK LAYER OF AIR   24

- The Air Around the Earth
- Up High
- Heavy Air and Light Air
- Dust in the Air
- Dirt in the Air
- Twinkling Stars

AIR DOES STRANGE THINGS 28

- Hot Air Goes Up
- Fire and Air
- Air Makes Things Move
- Air Is Transparent
- Air in Tanks
- Keeping Air Out

USING AIR EVERY DAY 32

- Air in Balloons
- Resting on Air
- Air in a Jackhammer
- Fans Make a Breeze
- Hot Air
- Air Can Help Cars Go Fast

AIR BRINGS US SOUNDS 36

- Blowing Air
- Talking
- Beating a Drum
- Other Sounds
- Hearing
- Sounds We Can't Hear

OUTER SPACE: WHERE THERE ISN'T ANY AIR 40

- Astronauts Living in Space Suits
- Flags Don't Move
- No Sound Anywhere
- The Black Sky
- It's Burning; It's Freezing
- Protection Without Air

GLOSSARY 42

INDEX 43

THE WIND

What Is Wind?

What happens when you open a window in your house on a breezy day? Papers fly around and doors slam. When you stand outside, your hair blows and you feel air moving against your face. This moving air is **wind**. Wind blows everywhere—out at sea, between mountains, even down the street where you live. Wind travels in every direction—north, south, east, and west.

Invisible Air

When the air isn't moving, there isn't any wind. When you are standing still and there is no wind, you don't feel the air. You can't see it or smell it. So it is easy to forget that air is everywhere around us. But when the air starts moving and the wind carries something away, like leaves or a kite, you immediately remember it. Sometimes the wind is very strong and sometimes it is very light. Can you feel any wind right now?

The Wind Makes Changes

Wind can change the shape of rocks, trees, and even mountains. In desert regions the wind picks up little pieces of sand and tosses them against rocks. Slowly the wind wears the rocks down. The wind also can blow a tree in one direction for so long that eventually the tree grows in that direction. Over many years, the wind can change the way the countryside looks.

A Windsock

This red and white **windsock** is like a big sleeve that the wind blows into. When a windsock fills with air, it points in the direction in which the wind is blowing. When the wind is blowing hard, it looks like the windsock in the picture. It is filled with air and stands straight out from the pole. When there is only a little wind, the windsock will hang limp. This shows how strongly the wind is blowing. Have you ever seen a windsock at an airport?

Sails Need Wind

The wind is often very strong in the middle of the ocean. That is because there is nothing to slow the wind down. There are no trees, mountains, or buildings. For sailors, the wind is very useful. When the wind blows into the sails of a sailboat, the boat is pushed along in the sea. Some sailboats have several very large sails. These boats can travel along the ocean very quickly during windy weather. Do you think the wind can push a boat without a sail?

Hurricanes

Over the ocean, very strong winds sometimes make large groups of clouds spin very fast. These clouds spin faster and faster around warm air. This giant spinning funnel-shaped cloud is called a **hurricane**. A **tornado** is like a hurricane except that it is much smaller and forms over the land. Both hurricanes and tornadoes can cause a lot of damage. They can easily destroy houses, trees, and ships.

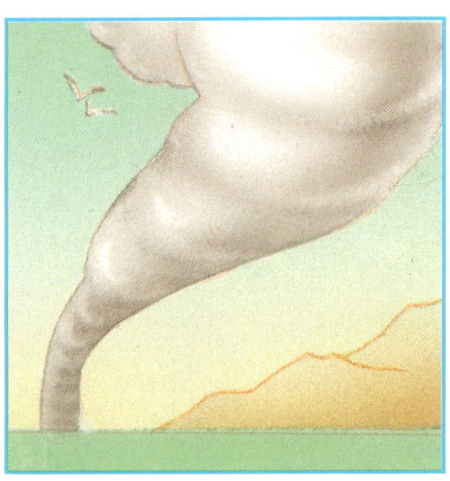

Do you think the wind makes it harder, or easier, for birds to fly?

AIR TRAVELERS

A Giant Kite

This enormous kite is called a hang-glider. A person is strapped to a frame, which is attached to the kite. The hang-glider is blown through the air by the wind. One way for people to fly is to hold onto something with wings, like this hang-glider. You can soar high above the land just like a bird. But even with a hang-glider, flying is dangerous. Never use a hang-glider unless you are with someone who has learned how to fly it!

Easy Flying

Everywhere you look on a windy day you see things taking off in the wind. Scraps of paper and string and bits of dirt all fly around. It only takes a **breeze** to lift these light things into the air. Why do you think people don't take off when there is a strong wind? What about the flowers in the picture? Do they fly away when the wind starts to blow?

Wings

Butterflies and birds fly by flapping their wings. Their wings are big enough and strong enough to get them off the ground. In the air they can go in any direction and move at any speed. They do this by changing the way they move their wings. People cannot fly the way birds do. Even if we strapped artificial wings to our bodies, they wouldn't be strong enough to keep us from falling.

Airplanes

Airplanes fly. But an airplane doesn't fly by flapping its wings like a bird. Airplanes fly by using powerful motors. These are attached to the airplane's wings. When these motors push the plane through the air, its large wings lift the airplane off the ground and keep it flying. The pilot can make the airplane go up or down, and turn right or left. He does this by raising or lowering little flaps at the edge of the wings. What other flying machines can you think of?

A Pointed Nose

Real airplanes have pointed noses like the paper airplane in the picture. Their noses help them fly. Think of birds. Their beaks are pointed, too. Having a pointed nose or beak helps things fly. This is because a pointed nose pushes air out of the way as you fly.

Falling Slowly

Have you ever seen seeds from a tree or flower floating through the air as in this picture? Whenever seeds fall, they are blown around in the air and fall very slowly. This is because they are so light that the air holds them up as they drop to the ground. Also, plants and flowers have tiny wings that help to slow them down. These wings are just like a parachute, which opens up to keep a person from falling too fast.

Look at the big picture. Which things in the picture can fly and which can't?

THE AIR WE BREATHE

What's in Air?

You can't catch air in your hands. That's because it isn't solid. You can't drink air from a glass. That's because it isn't liquid, either. Air is a **gas**. Air is really a mixture of several different gases. All of them are **transparent** and have no smell. The most important gas in air is **oxygen**. Oxygen is what we breathe. Another important gas in the air is **carbon dioxide**. This is the gas plants need in order to live.

Always Breathing

Imagine that you are sitting in the shade beside a lake. The sounds from the river are so peaceful that before you know it, you are asleep. But even when you are asleep, you are breathing. First you **inhale**, or breathe in air. Then you **exhale**, or breathe out. You cannot live if you do not keep breathing. And the gas you have to keep inhaling is oxygen. Oxygen keeps you alive. What else besides oxygen do we need to live?

Animals Breathe, Too

All animals have to breathe, too, just like people do. Horses, birds, lizards, even little beetles must inhale and exhale air to live. But not all animals breathe the same way. People have **lungs** to help them breathe. So do dogs and cats and mice. But some tiny creatures, like this beetle, breathe through their skin. Can you guess what other animals don't breathe the way we do? Can you guess why?

Fresh Air

People are inhaling air all day long. The gas that we need from the air is oxygen. What we don't need is carbon dioxide. This gas cannot be used by our bodies. If we stayed in a house with all the windows shut for many days, we would use up some of the oxygen. This is why it is important to open the windows sometimes to let in fresh air. Not only does it feel good but it is good for you, too!

Plants Need Air

Although plants don't breathe like people do, they need air, too. Plants use the carbon dioxide in the air in order to live. Carbon dioxide and sunshine combine to help plants make their own food. Plants take carbon dioxide out of the air and change it into oxygen. Helping to keep the air full of oxygen is something plants do for us.

Fish Don't Like Air

When a fish is caught and taken out of water, it starts to wriggle around. If the fisherman doesn't put it back in the water right away, the fish will die. This is because fish can't breathe in air. Fish need oxygen to live, but their lungs don't work in air. Their lungs are made for getting oxygen out of water. Unlike the fishes' lungs, our lungs do not get oxygen from water, but from the air. If we stayed underwater very long, we would not be able to breathe.

The air next to the river is cooler than the air in the nearby fields. Water cools the air near it. How do you think the sun affects the air?

WEATHER IN THE AIR

Hot Air and Cold Air

There are large pockets of air that circle the earth all the time. Air near the equator is hot. Air near the North and South Pole is cold. When a pocket of the cold or hot air moves, this is called an **air current**. Sometimes the hot and cold currents come close to each other. The result can be a storm, with rain, snow, or wind.

Water in the Air

When you go outside on a sunny day, you can't tell that there is water in the air. If it's not raining, you don't get wet. But there is always some water in the air, even though you can't see it or feel it. When enough water is present, tiny drops of water may be seen. We call this a cloud. When the cloud becomes filled with drops, the drops fall to the earth. This is what we call rain.

Beautiful Rainbows

Have you ever tried to stand by a rainbow? Have you tried to touch one with your hand? If you have, you know that it's impossible. A rainbow looks like a brightly colored ribbon in the sky. But it isn't. A rainbow is only light from the sun shining on tiny drops of water in the air. As soon as the drops of water fall from the sky or blow away in the wind, the rainbow disappears.

The Color of the Sky

Have you ever seen a sunset like the one in this picture? The sky is usually red when the sun sets. This is because light has farther to travel through the earth's atmosphere when the sun is low in the sky—both at sunrise and sunset. No other color can travel as far as red. Other colors are scattered before we can see them. Since red travels farthest, that makes the sky look red as the sun rises and sets.

A Flash of Lightning

Someone has painted a big **lightning** bolt on this balloon. It looks just like what you may have seen in the sky on a stormy night. In a real storm, a lightning bolt flashes out from some dark clouds. Then comes a loud crash of **thunder**. The lightning lights up the sky. Lightning is a very big spark of electricity. This spark flashes from cloud to cloud or between a cloud and the surface of the earth. Lightning can be dangerous, but it is also very beautiful.

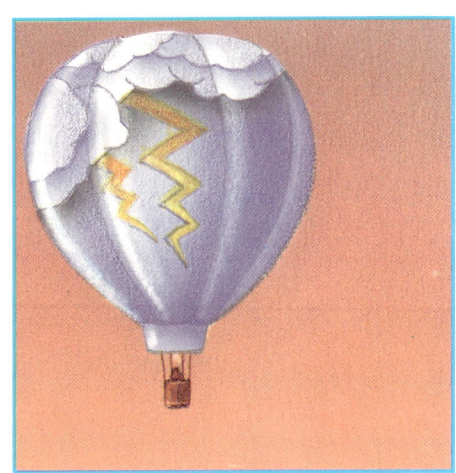

Weather Instruments

Traveling in a balloon is a lot of fun. But in a balloon, the changing weather is important. There are many different instruments that can help to tell us what the weather will be like. Attached to the basket of this balloon is an instrument that tells the speed of the wind. Another instrument, called a **thermometer**, tells us how hot or cold the air is. For what kinds of jobs is a good thermometer very important?

Did you see the stars in the night sky? We can't see them during the day because the sun is too bright. Why can't we see stars on a rainy night?

21

THE ATMOSPHERE: A THICK

The Air Around the Earth

There is a thick blanket of air over all the lands and all the seas of the earth. It covers everything from the food you eat to the ground you walk on. This air protects the earth in much the same way as a mitten protects your hand. During the day it keeps the sun from making the earth too hot. At night it protects the earth from getting too cold. This thick blanket of air is called the **atmosphere**.

Up High

The higher in the mountains you go, the colder the air becomes. If you went up very high, it would be hard to breathe. This is because the higher you go, the less air there is. Therefore, there is less oxygen. Because we need a lot of oxygen to live, we cannot go high in the sky without taking oxygen with us. Airplanes are specially made to hold enough oxygen for everyone to breathe no matter how high they fly.

Heavy Air and Light Air

This instrument is called a **barometer**. It is used to measure the weight of the air around it. A barometer helps people tell what the weather will be. If you look at the arrows on a barometer, they will give you an idea of whether it is going to be rainy or sunny.

LAYER OF AIR

Dust in the Air

Has a little bit of dust ever blown into your eye? If so, you know there are bits of dust in the air, even though you can't see them. Everywhere in the atmosphere there are tiny floating things. Some of these things are big enough to be seen. The seeds from flowers are carried by the wind. Can you think of other things that float in the atmosphere?

Dirt in the Air

There is more in the air than dust and seeds. The air can carry anything that is lightweight. It can carry a feather, or tiny insects. Whenever you burn wood in a fireplace, the smoke from the chimney is carried away in the air. Factories that make a lot of smoke also send dirt out into the air. It is important that we try to keep our air clean. Too much smoke in the air can make us sick. Why do you think the air is cleaner in the countryside than in the city?

Twinkling Stars

If you look at the sky on a clear night, you will see lots of stars. They look like tiny lights twinkling in the sky. But these stars are really very, very large. Stars are large balls of fire just like the sun. They look smaller than the sun because they are so far away. They aren't really twinkling, either. This is because bits of dust and tiny water drops sometimes block their light and make them seem to flicker.

Do you think the high air of the mountains makes as much difference to insects as it does to people?

AIR DOES STRANGE THINGS

Hot Air Goes Up

On a cold day we turn on the heat in our houses to keep us warm. Radiators, like the one shown here, heat up the air. Hot air, from a radiator or anywhere else, always rises. The hot air makes tiny air currents. These hot air currents move up, and carry with them anything light in the air. You can do an experiment to show that hot air rises. Put a little balloon above a hot radiator like the one in this picture. What happens?

Fire and Air

The candles on this birthday cake have not been lighted yet. But before you can light a match to light the candles, there has to be air. The oxygen in air is what keeps a flame burning. Without oxygen, nothing can burn— not a match, not candles, not even a fire in a fireplace. But don't worry—there is oxygen everywhere!

Air Makes Things Move

The little motor on a motorboat makes a lot of noise. The engine of a car makes a lot of noise, too. In a car's engine and a boat's motor, air is mixed with gasoline. Mixing the two together causes an explosion. This explosion causes the car or the boat to move. All things that move by motors, like airplanes and trucks, are using air to help them move. Can you think of other things that need air and gasoline to move?

Air Is Transparent

This child is looking through a pair of **binoculars**. Binoculars are special glasses used to see things that are far away. Binoculars make things that are far away look like they are very near. They are good for looking at birds in a tree or airplanes in the sky. When you look through binoculars, you can see a very long way and still see perfectly. This is because air is transparent.

Air in Tanks

These little toy dolls are dressed up like sea divers. Sea divers swim in the deepest part of the oceans to observe marine life. But there isn't very much oxygen underwater. To breathe underwater, divers have to carry oxygen with them in special tanks. The tanks have a special faucet and pipe attached to them. The divers breathe the oxygen through the pipe as they swim along.

Keeping Air Out

The peanuts in the picture are in a plastic bag. This bag has no air inside. All the air was forced out by a special machine in a factory. Food rots if you leave it in the air for too long. By keeping food away from air, it helps the food to stay fresh. What do you think happens to half an apple if you leave it out in the air for a long time?

Did you notice the frosting on the cake and the pudding in the glasses in the big picture? Both need to be mixed with air to be light and delicious.

USING AIR EVERY DAY

Air in Balloons

What happens when you blow into a balloon? The balloon **inflates**, or fills up with air. You can keep blowing air into the balloon until the balloon is full. Then you can tie a knot in the end of the balloon. Or you can let all the air out again. If you keep blowing more air into the balloon after it is full, something will happen. Can you guess what it is?

Resting on Air

Look at the tires on this toy car. They are like little balloons or pillows that the car rests on. The tires are filled with air. Inflated tires keep the car moving smoothly and evenly, even over bumpy roads. Sometimes a tire gets a hole in it and loses all its air. The tire **deflates**. Have you ever tried to ride a bike with a flat tire? If you have, you know how much easier it is when the tire is filled with air.

Air in a Jackhammer

This worker is using a jackhammer. A jackhammer is a large, powerful hammer. It can break through a sidewalk easily. Inside this machine, trapped air pushes the big hammer up and down very fast. The trapped air does the work of three or four people.

Fans Make a Breeze

This little girl is holding a fan. Fans are very useful for moving air. When air moves, it makes a little breeze. Air moving slowly over our face can cool us down when we're hot. But air is even more useful when it is moving very fast. Big fans that move air very fast cool us down very quickly.

Hot Air

This girl has painted a design on the balloon. She is drying the paint with a hair dryer. This is faster than letting it dry by itself. The air outside will dry anything, but the hotter the air the quicker things dry. That's why when you get out of a pool on a hot day your skin dries very quickly.

Air Can Help Cars Go Fast

The colored lines around this car show how air moves over an object. The shape of a car will affect the way the air moves over it. A sleek, slim car that is low to the ground, such as a sports car, will move very fast because the air can quickly skim over and around it. A large gasoline tanker will move much more slowly. Can you guess why?

Look at the big picture of the classroom. Do you think the air is colder inside, or outside?

AIR BRINGS US SOUNDS

Blowing Air

You have to blow air through a recorder if you want a sound to come out. Without air, there isn't any sound. By covering different holes with your fingers and blowing, you will make different sounds. The more air you blow into the recorder, the louder the sound will be.

Talking

Everyone likes to talk. But to talk you need air. In the back of your throat, you have a tiny **voice box**. Every time you make a sound, you are using it. In the voice box are very little cords. When you talk, air passes over these cords and they **vibrate** to make sounds. The air carries these sounds in waves. The loudness or softness of sounds depends on the number of vibrations per second.

Beating a Drum

A drum also makes sounds because of air. Inside a drum there is trapped air. When you hit the top of a drum with drumsticks, the top vibrates. This causes the air inside the drum to be bounced around. This trapped moving air is what makes the beating sound of a drum.

Other Sounds

Outside there are many different sounds. Cars, people, dogs—even the wind, the air itself, make sounds. If you don't want to hear these sounds, just close the windows. All sounds are carried by the air. If you shut the air out, you shut the sound out, too. It is difficult for sounds to get through a closed door. This is because it is difficult for the air to get through. When you close a door to a noisy room, often you can still hear some sounds. Why?

Hearing

Just as air carries sounds to us, it also allows us to hear. Sounds are carried into your ears by the air. When the air arrives deep inside your ear, it causes a few tiny bones to vibrate. When these vibrate, they make the sound carried by the air louder so that you can hear it. The little bones in some people's ears don't work. They can't hear any noise at all. People who can't hear are deaf, or hearing-impaired.

Sounds We Can't Hear

Bats usually fly at night. They have poor eyesight and can see almost nothing, so daylight does not help them. Instead, bats use their voices to guide them when they fly. They have a strange little squeak that can be heard by all other bats but not by people. Our ears cannot hear because air vibrates differently in different animals' ears. In this way, different animals can hear different sounds.

Look at the instruments in the big picture. Can you guess how air helps each instrument make a sound?

OUTER SPACE: WHERE THERE

Astronauts Living in Space Suits

Far from the earth, out in space, there isn't any air, or atmosphere. Because there isn't oxygen in space, astronauts have to wear special space suits. These suits have special tanks of oxygen attached to them. These tanks are similar to the ones divers use underwater. By carrying oxygen with them, astronauts can stay in space for a long time. In their space shuttle, there is also oxygen for them to breathe.

Flags Don't Move

Without air there can be no wind. This means that if you hang a flag in space, it won't flap in a breeze. It won't move at all. Astronauts attach sticks to the flag so that the flag will hang straight out. On the earth, flags flap because there is the plenty of air to move them around. What happens to a flag on the earth when you put it outside on a windless day?

No Sound Anywhere

We know that sounds are carried in the air. We also know that we hear sounds only with the help of air. So what happens to sounds in space? Do the space shuttle's engines make a sound? The answer is no. There is no sound in space, because there is no air to carry the sound. When astronauts travel in space, they hear nothing. If the astronauts want to talk to each other, they have to talk inside the shuttle where there is air to carry their voices.

ISN'T ANY AIR

The Black Sky

During the day on earth, light from the sun lights up the sky, the clouds, and everything else around us. We know that on earth the tiny pieces of dust and water in the air catch the sun's light. But in space everything is dark. The sky is always black, even during the day! This is because with no atmosphere, there is nothing in space to catch the sun's light.

It's Burning; It's Freezing

With no atmosphere, there is nothing to protect things in space. The sun is so strong that when it shines on the few things that are there, they become burning hot. In the shade, away from the sun's light, it is so cold that things freeze. Because of the changes in temperature, space shuttles and the astronauts must be well prepared. Both the shuttle and the astronauts' space suits must be able to **insulate** the astronauts from the changing temperatures.

Protection Without Air

The sun can be very dangerous in space. It is so bright that it can burn your eyes. If the astronauts looked at the sun without their helmets on, their eyes would be badly damaged. They would not be able to see again. The helmets the astronauts wear have special sunglasses attached to them that protect their eyes. By wearing these, they can travel in space without worrying—almost as if they were back on earth!

41

GLOSSARY

AIR CURRENT	A pocket of air that moves around the earth. *A warm* air current *gives us warm weather and a cold* air current *gives us cold weather.*
ATMOSPHERE	The thick blanket of air that covers and protects the earth.
BAROMETER	An instrument used to measure the weight of the air around it. *A barometer helps people tell what the weather will be.*
BINOCULARS	Special glasses used to see things that are far away.
BREEZE	A light wind.
CARBON DIOXIDE	A gas present in the air around us that has no color or smell. *Carbon dioxide is the gas that plants need in order to live.*
DEFLATES	Lets the air out of something.
EXHALE	To breathe out. *You* exhale *carbon dioxide when you blow air out of your mouth and nose.*
GAS	A substance that is neither solid nor liquid. *Steam from a kettle is a gas.*
HURRICANE	A storm with very strong winds spinning around a center of warm air. Hurricanes *always develop over the ocean.*
INFLATES	Fills up with air.
INHALE	To breathe in. *You* inhale *oxygen when you take a deep breath.*
INSULATE	To stop hot or cold temperatures from going in or out of something.
LIGHTNING	A very big spark of electricity that flashes from cloud to cloud or between a cloud and the surface of the earth.
LUNGS	The part of your body that helps you breathe. Lungs *help your body use the oxygen that you inhale.*
OXYGEN	A gas present in the air around us that has no color or smell. Oxygen *is the gas that people must breathe in order to live.*
THERMOMETER	An instrument that tells us how hot or cold the air is.
THUNDER	The loud noise made when lightning flashes.
TORNADO	Very strong, fast spinning winds turning in a funnel shape. While much smaller than hurricanes, they can still do a lot of damage. Tornadoes *develop over the land.*
TRANSPARENT	Anything that can be seen through. *Glass is* transparent.
VIBRATE	To move up and down or from side to side quickly.
VOICE BOX	The part of your throat where sounds are made by air moving over little cords.
WIND	Moving air that blows in every direction. *The weather depends on the way the* wind *blows.*
WINDSOCK	A big sleeve that the wind blows into. When filled with air, it points in the direction in which the wind is blowing.

INDEX

A

Air
   blowing, 36
   composition of, 16
   dust and dirt in, 25
   fire and, 28
   fresh, 17
   hot and cold, 20, 28, 33
   invisible, 8
   keeping out, 29
   resting on, 32
   to make things move, 28, 33
   water in, 20
   weight of, 24
Air current, 20, 42
Airplanes, 13
Animals, 16
Astronauts, 40
Atmosphere, 24–25, 42

B

Balloon, 21, 32
Barometer, 24, 42
Binoculars, 29, 42
Breathing, 16–17
Breeze, 12, 33, 42

C

Carbon dioxide, 16, 17, 42

D

Deflation, 32, 42
Dirt, 25
Drum, 36
Dust, 25

E

Exhalation, 16, 42

F

Fans, 33
Fire, 28
Fish, 17
Flags, 40

G

Gas, 16, 42

H

Hang-glider, 12
Hearing, 37
Hurricane, 9, 42

I

Inflation, 32, 42
Inhalation, 16, 17, 42
Insulation, 41, 42

J

Jackhammer, 32

L

Lightning, 21, 42
Lungs, 16, 42

O

Outer space, 40–41
Oxygen, 16, 17, 24, 29, 42

P

Plants, 17

R

Rainbows, 20

S

Sails, 9
Sky color, 21, 41
Sound, 36–37, 40
Stars, 25
Sun, 41

T

Talking, 36
Thermometer, 21, 42
Thunder, 21, 42
Tornado, 9, 42
Transparency, 16, 29, 42

V

Vibration, 36, 42
Voice box, 36, 42

W

Water, 20
Weather, 20–21
Wind, 8–9, 42
Windsock, 9, 42
Wings, 12–13